Quiet In My Body

Frustrated and Calm

I'm getting dressed all on my own today:

First, I put on my favorite stripey shorts, then my T. rex tee shirt. Next, I put on my shades—that's what Uncle Dwayne calls sunglasses—and my flip flops.

I look pretty sharp! I'm going to the park today to play with my friends. I've been waiting all week.

3

"Let's go!" I say to Mama.

She smiles. "Gio, it's pretty cold outside. I think you need some warmer clothes."

"I got all dressed."

"I see that. You did a marvelous job. The thing is, the weather today is blustery, which means it's cold and windy."

My tummy starts feeling twisty.
I squeeze my elbow with my fingers
and I feel tears. I was all dressed!

"Honey, I just want you to be
comfortable so we don't have to
go home early when you get cold."

"I won't get cold," I say.

My voice gets loud and then quiet
again, like it can't decide how to be.

Mama comes over and rubs my back.

"You look like you're feeling really frustrated," she says.

"I understand that. I would feel frustrated, too. I do think we can solve this problem and still go to the park, if you're willing to make a couple of new choices about your outfit."

"I have a much easier time solving problems when I feel calm," Mama says.

"Would you like me to help you feel calm? I always start with my breathing."

Mama and I lie down on the floor and she holds my hand. For a minute, I think I might want to pull my hand away, but I don't; her hand is soft and warm.

"First, I breathe in slowly through my nose—one, two, three, four—and then out again through my mouth—one, two, three, four, five. Shall we do it together?"

I try breathing slowly, like Mama. I feel my body getting still. It's nice.

I close my eyes and feel my tummy go up and down with my breathing. "I feel quiet in my body," I say.

"Good. That sounds like the feeling of being calm. Now you're ready to make some new choices about your clothes so you can go to the park."

Mama stands up and holds out her hands to help me up, too.

"Let's go outside and feel the weather. You can decide how cold it is."

We stand outside for a little while. My toes get cold first, and then the chilly wind blows right inside my tee shirt.

I have goosebumps on my legs!

Mama is right: it's too cold to wear this. We go back inside.

"What do you think, Gio?" Mama asks.
"Soft pants or jeans? Your choice."

"Soft pants," I answer.

I take off my stripey shorts and put
on my green joggers instead.

"Let's put some long sleeves under your T. rex shirt, and add your coat on top to keep you warm," Mama says. "Can you show me your coat flip?"

"Yes! I can do it all by myself."

I put my coat on the floor, put my hands in the sleeves, and flip it over my head.

I need a little bit of help with my socks, but I can do my shoes all on my own.

"Now I'm ready," I say to Mama.

23

"Well, almost," she says, and hands me my shades.

I put them on and look at myself in the mirror.

I look pretty sharp!

Can you find a page where Gio felt frustrated?

Can you make a frustrated face?

When have you felt frustrated?